The Little Safari Animals

Written and Illustrated
by Steven Ward

The little safari animals walked into the jungle, looking for an adventure into the mysterious, vast wilderness.

Into the jungle past the tallest trees, into the thorny bushes, and across the green fields.

After reaching the deepest part of the jungle and searching every bush, safari friends were missing.

A clumsy little monkey, A curious donkey, and a round little elephant were not there.

Where in the humid wilderness is the safari animals?

They pondered, for their safari friends were not in the deepest part of the wilderness.

The safari animals were not at the top of the tallest tree.

The safari animals were not at the top of the second-tallest tree.

As soon as the safari animals peered out into the vast wilderness, past the thorny bushes and green fields was a tribe of clumsy monkeys pondering the whereabouts of the little clumsy monkey.

The clumsy little monkey was not deep into the wilderness and not at the top of the tallest tree.

"Why is everyone acting so weird?" The funny-looking bird asked the clumsy little monkey.

Up from the wilderness, the little safari animals went zing, zip, zoom till they reached exciting new places; there were the safari animals.

"Where in the vast, humid safari did everyone go?" Has everyone just gone wild?" The safari animals asked.

"We visited great places." Then the clumsy little monkey fell out of the spaceship". Said the safari animals.

Then the puzzled safari animals started to look around and gaze, and they saw it too.

"Spaceships." the safari animals yelled.

Up from the wilderness, the little safari animals went zing, zip, zoom till they reached the North Atlantic Ocean.

Down past the jungle, above the tallest trees, into the water, and deep into the North Atlantic Ocean.

The safari animals
were so excited.

Up from the North Atlantic Ocean, the little safari animals went zing, zip, and zoom till they reached the pyramids of Egypt.

Beyond the jungle, above the tallest trees, into the North Atlantic Ocean, and deep into the pyramids of Egypt.

The safari animals
were so excited.

Home they went, zing, zip, and zoom. Beyond the Egyptian pyramids, out of the North Atlantic Ocean, above the tallest trees, and back into the jungle one after the other.

The little safari animals traveled the deepest parts of the jungle, found big adventures, and made many friends!

The END

9 798361 478064